All The Best

FOR PIANO

A Treasury of Hymns, Gospel Songs, and Praise & Worship Favorites

25

Arrangements by

Cindy Berry • Roger House • Gail Smith • Stan Pethel • Teresa Wilhelmi
Don Phillips • Tim Conyers • Jeff Bennett • Lavawan Riley

Lillenas PUBLISHING COMPANY
Kansas City, MO 64141

Contents

Give Thanks

HENRY SMITH
Arranged by Roger House

Moderately

6

Happily

It Is Well with My Soul

PHILIP P. BLISS
Arranged by Lavawan Riley

Calm and Slow ♩ = ca. 54

Jesus, the Very Thought of Thee

In the setting of *Jesu, Joy of Man's Desiring*

JOHN B. DYKES
Arranged by Cindy Berry

Lord, We Praise You (Medley)

O Come, Let Us Adore Him
Lord, We Praise You

Arranged by Jeff Bennett

16

*"Lord, We Praise You"

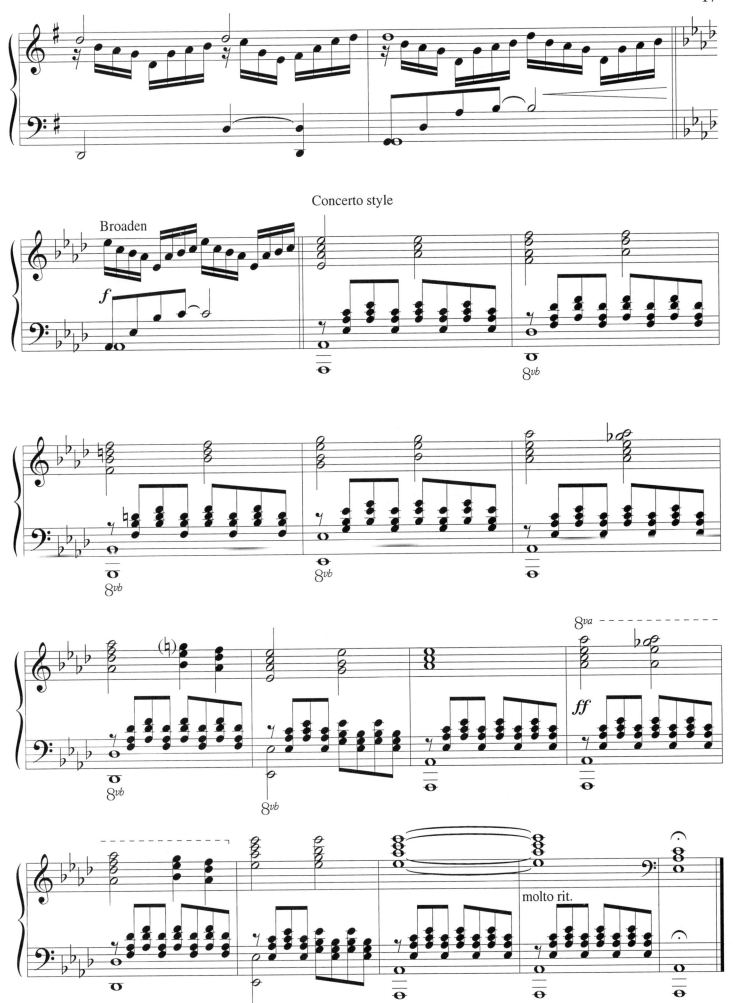

Holy Ground

GERON DAVIS
Arranged by Tim Conyers

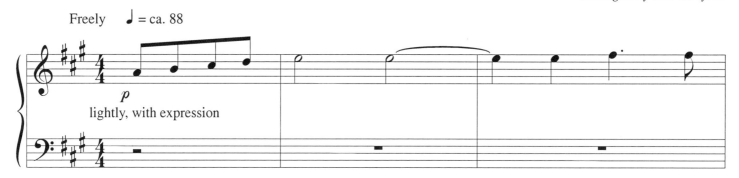

Christ the Lord Is Risen Today

In the setting of G. F. Handel's *Hallelujah* from <u>The Messiah</u>

From *Lyra Davidica*, 1708
Arranged by Gail Smith

Crown Him with Many Crowns

In the setting of J. S. Bach's *Prelude in D Major*

GEORGE ELVEY
Arranged by Cindy Berry

Andante ♩ = ca. 76

cresc. poco a poco

For the Beauty of the Earth

With
This Is My Father's World

CONRAD KOCHER
Arranged by Teresa Wilhelmi

Vivace

Warmer, smoother

rit.

Very rubato

accel.

*"This Is My Father's World"

Blessed Assurance

PHOEBE PALMER KNAPP
Arranged by Jeff Bennett

Lamb of Glory

GREG NELSON and PHILL MCHUGH
Arranged by Stan Pethel

Moderately, with expression

Near to the Heart of God

With expression

CLELAND B. MCAFEE
Arranged by Roger House

O Love That Wilt Not Let Me Go

ALBERT L. PEACE
Arranged by Don Phillips

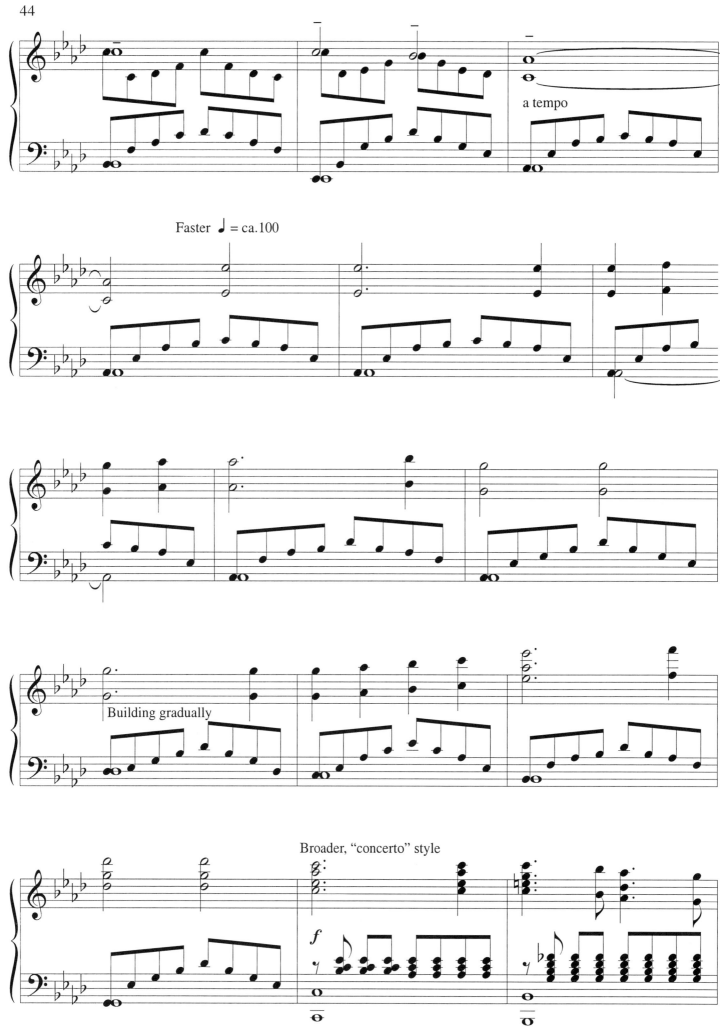

Moment by Moment

In the setting of Camille Saint-Saëns' *Le Cygne*

MAY WHITTLE MOODY
Arranged by Cindy Berry

Slowly, with expression   ♩ = ca. 80

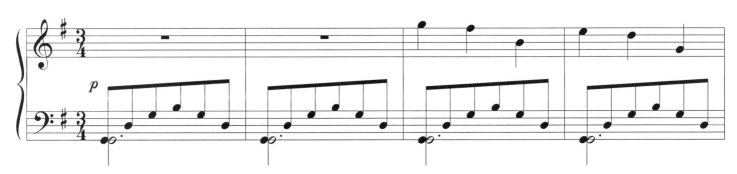

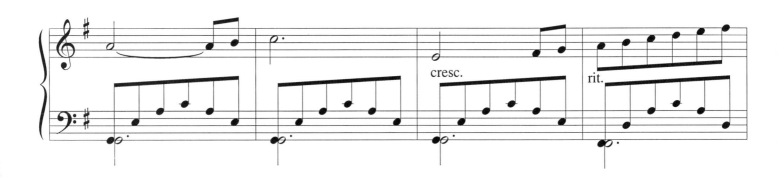

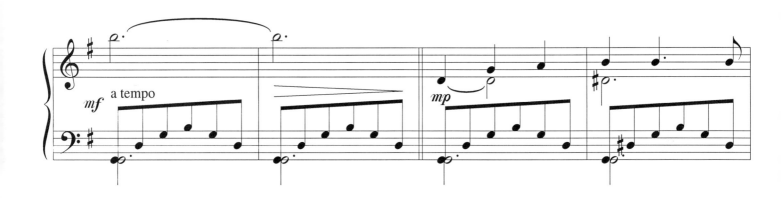

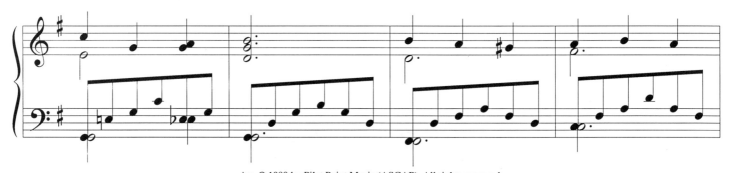

O the Deep, Deep Love of Jesus

In the setting of Ludwig van Beethoven's *Moonlight Sonata, 1st Movement, Op. 27, No. 3*

THOMAS J. WILLIAMS
Arranged by Gail Smith

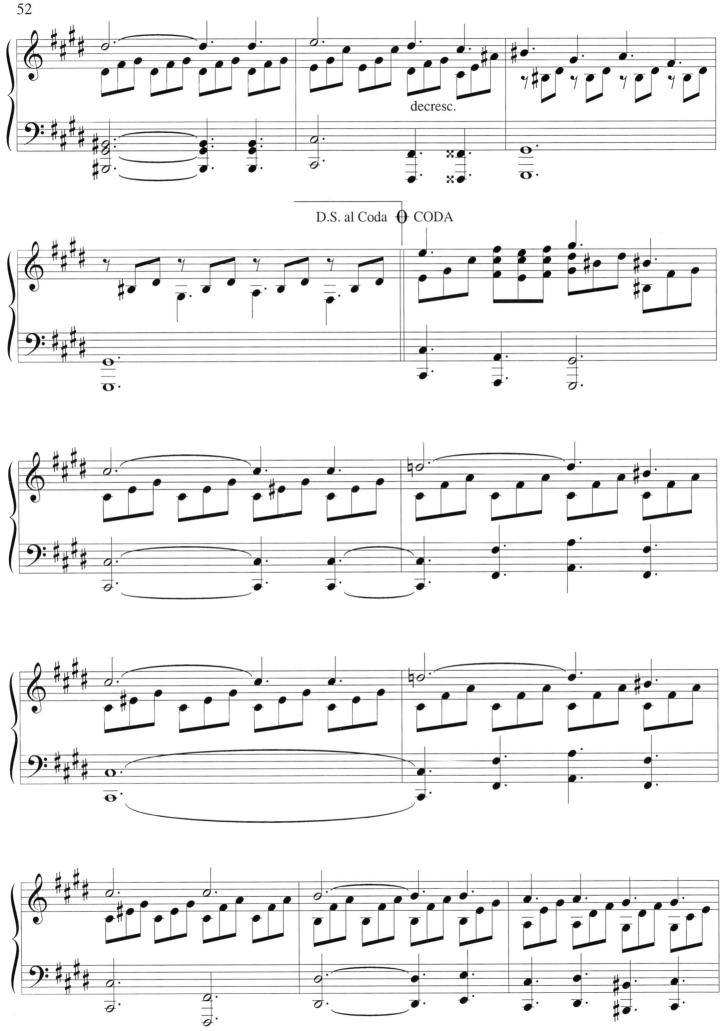

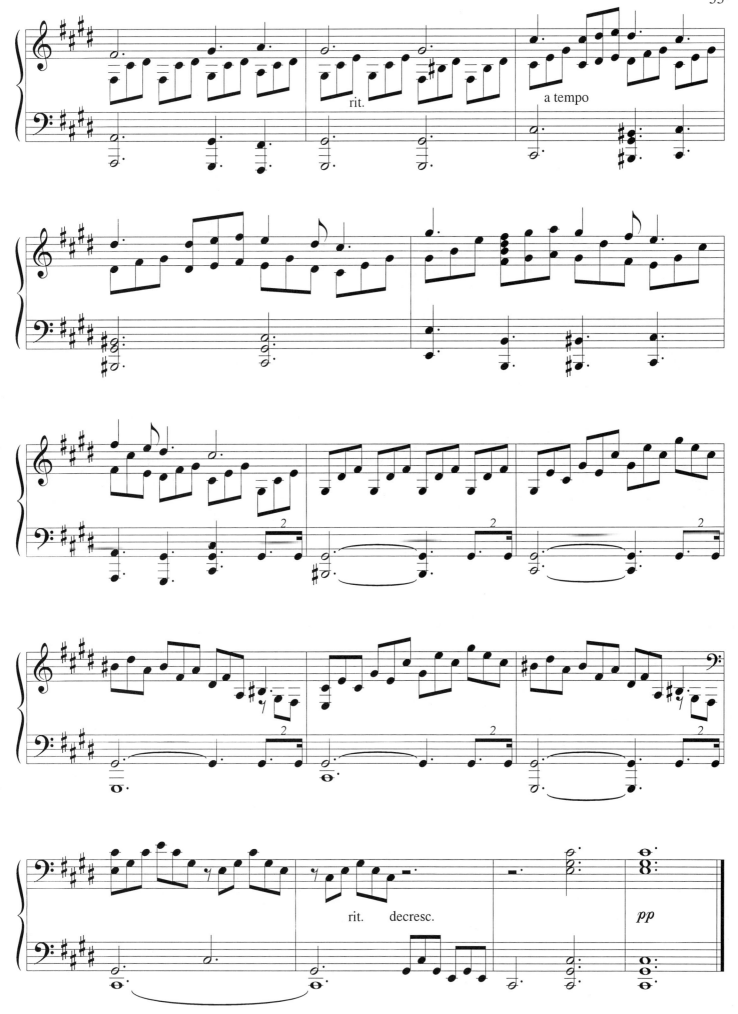

Praise to the Lord, the Almighty

from *Stralsund Gesangbuch*
Arranged by Roger House

Evenly, not too fast

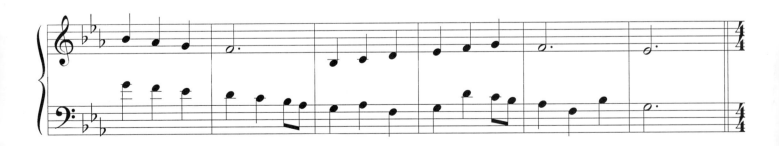

What a Friend We Have in Jesus

CHARLES C. CONVERSE
Arranged by Lavawan Riley

Slowly and freely ♩ = ca. 54

How Majestic Is Your Name

With
Holy, Holy, Holy, Lord God Almighty

MICHAEL W. SMITH
Arranged by Stan Pethel

*"Holy, Holy, Holy, Lord God Almighty"

Smoothly

(.vallo.)

On Jordan's Stormy Banks

In the setting of W. A. Mozart's *Rondo Alla Turka*

Traditional American Melody
Arranged by Cindy Berry

Close to Thee

SILAS J. VAIL
Arranged by Don Phillips

Since Jesus Came into My Heart

CHARLES H. GABRIEL
Arranged by Roger House

Slightly slower

Break Thou the Bread of Life

In the setting of J.S. Bach's *Prelude in C*

WILLIAM F. SHERWIN
Arranged by Cindy Berry

Allegro

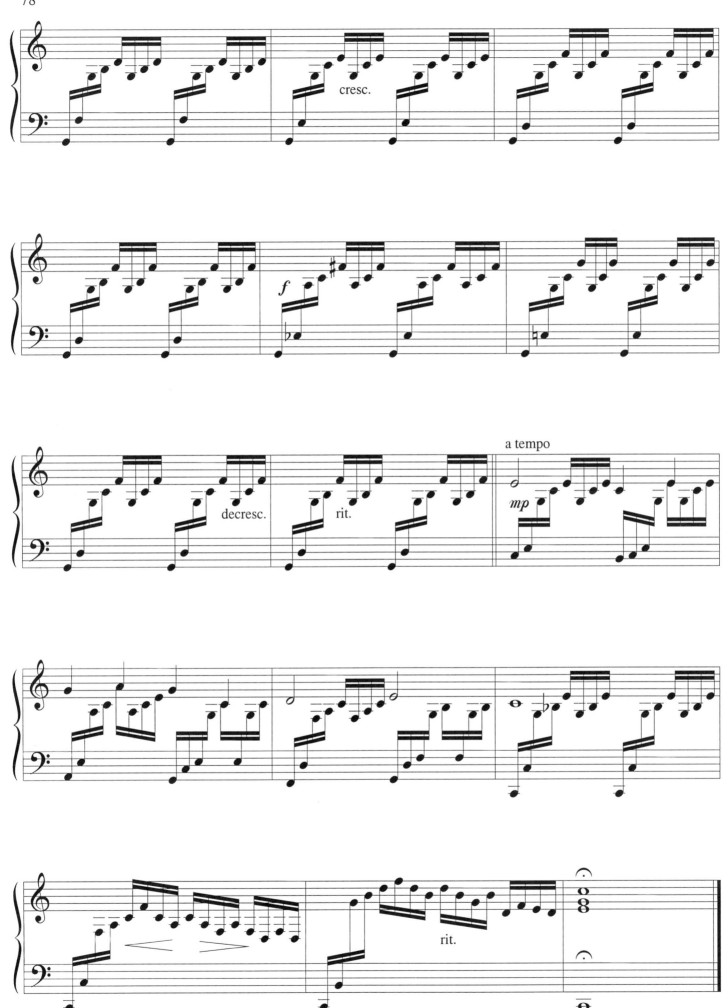

My Jesus, I Love Thee

ADONIRAM J. GORDON
Arranged by Don Phillips

As the Deer

MARTIN NYSTROM
Arranged by Roger House

Slowly, reverently

Sometimes I Feel Like a Motherless Child

Spiritual
Arranged by Teresa Wilhelmi

Slowly, with much expression

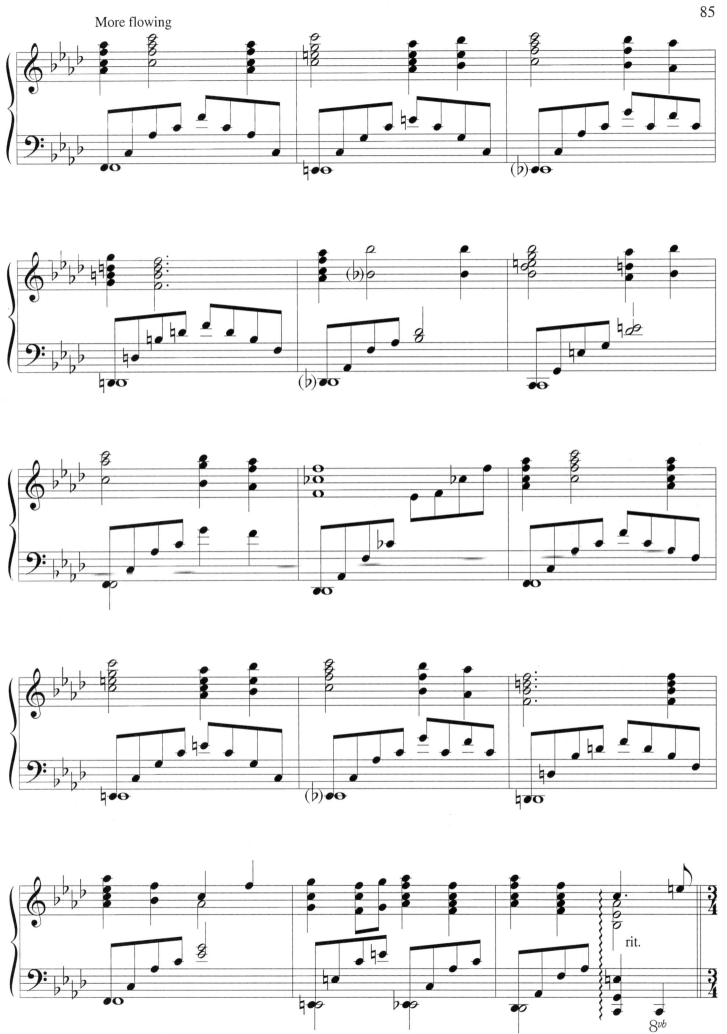

Waltz feel

We're Marching to Zion

In the setting of Franz Joseph Haydn's *Sonata in G Major*

ROBERT LOWRY
Arranged by Cindy Berry

Allegretto

CLASSICAL HYMNS

Piano Arrangements by Cindy Berry
An exciting collection of 14 traditional hymns combined with classical favorites. Moderate. Titles include: "Christ the Lord Is Risen Today"; "He Leadeth Me"; "I Will Sing of My Redeemer."   MB-727

HYMNS WITH A CLASSICAL TOUCH

Piano Arrangements by Cindy Berry
11 hymns and gospel songs with classical favorites in these terrific piano solos. Moderate. Titles include: "I Surrender All"; "Great Is Thy Faithfulness"; "It Is Well with My Soul."   MB-596

ALONE WITH GOD

Devotional Arrangements for Piano Solo with Hymn Texts, Scriptures, and Prayers
By Don Phillips
13 unique hymn arrangements designed for both corporate and personal worship. Moderate. Titles include: "Be Still, My Soul"; "I Need Thee Every Hour"; "What a Friend We Have in Jesus."   MB-619

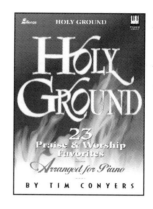

HOLY GROUND

23 Praise and Worship Favorites
Arranged for Piano by Tim Conyers
A treasury of contemporary favorites arranged sequentially in related keys or including modulations to allow for smooth transitions between thematically related songs. Moderate. Titles include: "Oh, the Glory of Your Presence"; "Forever Grateful"; "In Heaven's Eyes"; "He Is Able."   MB-759

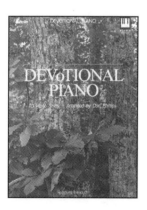

DEVOTIONAL PIANO

Arranger Don Phillips
10 hymns and gospel songs that are meditative and devotional in character, thus particularly appropriate for the Lenten season. Moderate. Titles include: "God So Loved the World"; "O Jesus, I Have Promised"; "I Saw the Cross of Jesus."   MB-577

THE LOVE OF GOD

Hymns of Faith and Assurance
Arranged by Lavawan Riley
10 songs for solo piano in a style that is traditional, yet fresh, tasteful, and expressive. Moderate. Titles include: "A Mighty Fortress Is Our God"; Great Is Thy Faithfulness"; "Amazing Grace."   MB-783

LORD, WE PRAISE YOU

Hymns and Praise Songs
Arranged for Solo Piano by Jeff Bennett
14 hymns, gospel songs, and praise songs in 10 unique arrangements. Moderate. Titles include: "All That Thrills My Soul"; "My Jesus, I Love Thee"; "Wonderful Words of Life." MB-714